A Happy Day® Book Collection

Favorite Bible Stories

from the Old Testament

Standard® PUBLISHING

Cincinnati, Ohio

A Happy Day® Book Collection

Contents

A long time ago,
There was nothing at all.
No world, sun, or creatures,
No people, big or small.

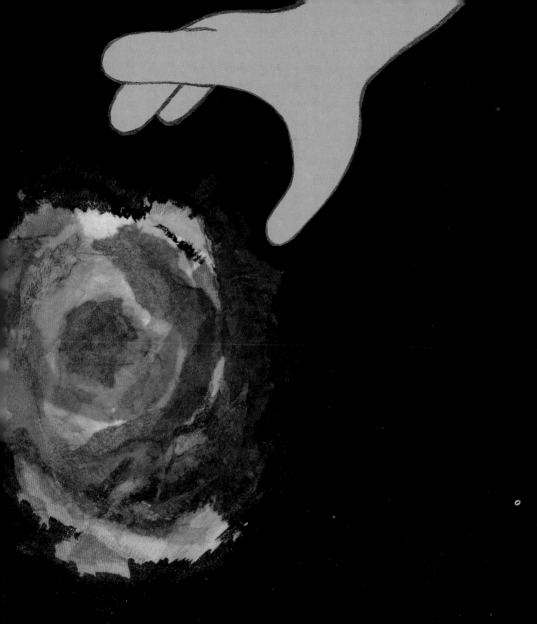

But God had a wonderful plan.
"I'll create the universe," God said,
    "and then I'll make a man."
And God did.

On the first day of creation,
God spoke and made daylight
   so bright,
And darkness, called night.
And God liked the daylight
   and darkness he had made.

On the second day of creation,
God spoke again.
God made the big, blue sky.
And God liked the big, blue sky he had made.

9

On the third day of
   creation,
God made the oceans,
   lakes, and seas,
And the dry land and
   growing trees.
And God liked the
   oceans, lakes, seas,
   and trees he had
   made.

On the fourth day of creation,
God made the sun so bright to shine
   in the day,
And the moon and stars to keep
   darkness away.
And God liked the sun, moon, and
   stars he had made.

On the fifth day of creation,
God made some sea creatures
big, and some very small.

He made birds of
every color, who fly
but never fall.
And God liked the sea
creatures and birds
he had made.

On the sixth day of creation,
God made all kinds of animals
    to live on the land,
And then last of all, God made
    a man.
And God liked the animals and
    the man he had made.

The man God made was Adam.
And Adam was all alone.

"I'll make a woman to help you," God said.
And he did from Adam's rib bone!

And God loved Adam and Eve, the first people on earth.

God made a beautiful garden
And gave it to Adam and Eve.
"This garden is yours to live
in," God said.
"If you obey, you'll never have
to leave."
And God liked the Garden of
Eden he had made.

On the seventh day,
God said, "I'm done . . . I've made what I should.
My creation is beautiful.
It's all very good."
Then God rested on the seventh day because his
    work of creation was done.

I'm glad that God created
Everything we can see.
But most of all I'm glad
That he loves even me!

Thank you, God.

God looked down from Heaven.
"Look at my people," he said sadly.
"They have forgotten all about me.
They are very bad."

But there was one man on the earth who was very
good. His name was Noah. Noah loved God very much.
Noah made God happy.

Hurry up, Noah, and listen to God!

One day God said to Noah, "I want you to make a big, big boat. I will tell you just how to do it."

So God told Noah just how big to make the boat.

Hurry up, Noah, and build the boat!

Noah built the boat just like God told him to do.
Hurry up, Noah, and obey God's Word!
Then God said, "Noah, I want you to take with you
two of every kind of animal and bird on the earth." Noah
made sure there was plenty of food for all of the animals
and his family too.

How busy Noah must have been! But soon he was finished. Then into the big boat went the sneaking snails and tiptoeing turtles. Two by two came the lumbering lions and prancing ponies. Marching monkeys and walking wolves filled the boat—just like God said. Then Noah and his family went into the big boat. God closed the door.

Hurry up, Noah, and fill the boat!

Rain! **Rain! RAIN!**

For 40 days and 40 nights, rain fell from the sky. Soon water covered the earth. But Noah and his family were safe and dry in the boat.

Hurry up, Noah, and see the rain!

For many days the boat floated on the water. Noah and his family were busy inside the boat taking care of the animals. *Hurry up, Noah, and feed the elephants!*

Woooo! ***Woooo! WOOOO!***

Do you hear the wind? God sent a big wind to dry up the water.

Hurry up, Noah, and listen to the wind!

Down! **Down! DOWN** went the boat as the water slowly dried up.

One day Noah sent a dove out. He wanted to see if the dove could find dry land. But the land was still covered with water, so the dove flew back into the boat.

Seven days later Noah sent the dove out again. This time the dove brought back a brand-new olive leaf. Seven days later Noah sent the dove out again. The dove flew away and did not come back. Then Noah knew that the dove had found a dry place to land.

Hurry up, Noah, and see the dry land!

Soon the earth was completely dry.

"Noah," God said, "it is time for you to leave the boat."

Hurry up, Noah, and leave the boat!

Out of the boat went leaping leopards and slithering snakes. Skipping skunks and jumping jackrabbits left the big boat. Dancing deer and racing raccoons followed. All of the animals and Noah's family were glad to be out on God's clean earth.

Hurry up, Noah, it's time to thank God!

Noah and his family built an altar to God. "Thank you, God," they said, "for keeping us safe."

God was pleased with his new earth, and he made a promise to Noah. "Never again will I send a big flood to cover the earth," God said.

Hurry up, Noah, and see God's rainbow!

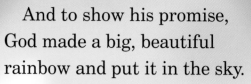

And to show his promise,
God made a big, beautiful
rainbow and put it in the sky.
    Noah was glad he had
obeyed God.

Abraham Trusts God

See the rocky road winding
away from the town?

38

39

When Abraham saw the rocky road, he heard God say, "This is the path you should go down." Abraham believed God's way was best so he made the journey to a new, strange place.

See the herdsman crossing the plain? See the tents pitched under the trees?

When Abraham saw the plain and the trees, he said to Lot, "God has given us such good land. There is more than enough for both of us."

See the sheep grazing on the shady hill? See the cattle drinking at the stream?

When Abraham saw the sheep and cattle, he said, "These are the riches God has given to me." Abraham was thankful for God's good gifts so he built an altar to worship God.

See the night, cloudless and dark? See the sky full of stars?

When God showed Abraham the night sky and the stars, Abraham saw God's promise to bless the whole world through Abraham. He trusted God's promise to give him a son.

See the wife with wrinkles around her eyes? See the husband with hair faded to white?

When Abraham saw the wrinkles and the white hair he laughed, "Sarah and I are too old to have a baby!"

See the boy on his mother's lap? See how the mother laughs with joy?

When Abraham saw the boy, he saw God's words coming true. The boy was Abraham's son, Isaac.

Abraham said, "I trust you, God.
You provide everything I need."

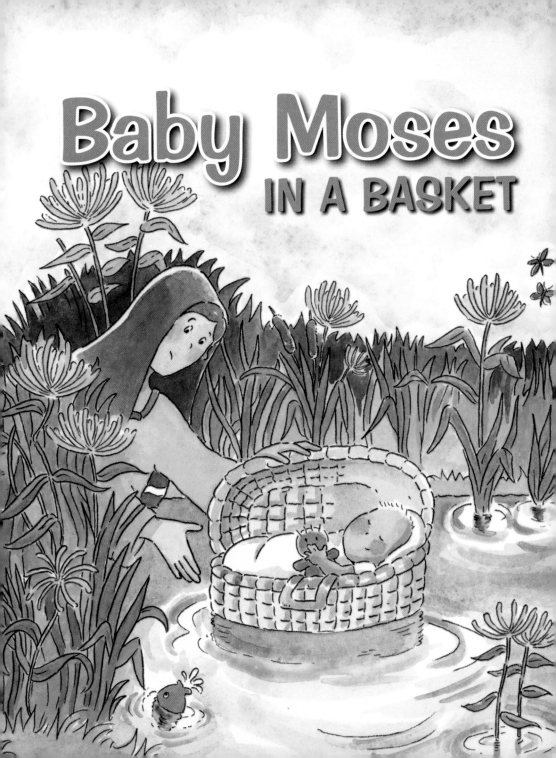

Miriam and Aaron had a baby brother. When their baby brother was born, their mother and dad said, "God has given us a beautiful baby boy. But we must keep him a secret. Pharaoh, the ruler of Egypt, wants to kill all of the Hebrew baby boys."

Miriam and Aaron loved their baby brother. They liked to play with him, sing to him, and smile at him.

But they had to be very quiet. They did not want Pharaoh's soldiers to find their baby brother.

One day their mother said, "Children, I am sorry, but we cannot hide our little baby any longer."

Miriam and Aaron started to cry. "Mother, you don't mean we have to give our brother to the mean Pharaoh?"

"No," said Mother. "God has given me a plan. God will help us take care of our baby. But I need your help." Quietly, Mother told them what to do.

Mother made a little basket. "It will float on water," she said. "It will keep our baby safe."

Carefully, Mother wrapped their little brother in a blanket and laid him in the basket.

Miriam and her mother walked down to the Nile River. Very quietly, and oh so carefully, Mother put the basket in the water.

"Miriam," Mother whispered, "watch your little brother. If anything happens to him, come and tell me just as fast as you can."

Miriam hid in the tall grass. She watched the little basket floating in the water. The water was very gentle. "Dear God," she whispered, "please keep my little brother safe."

As Miriam stood watching, Pharaoh's daughter, the princess, came down to take a bath in the river.

One of the princess' servants went into the water and picked up the basket. The princess opened the little basket and Miriam's baby brother began to cry.

"Oh, what a pretty baby!" the princess said. "He will be my son."

Miriam quickly left her hiding place and ran to the princess. "Would you like for me to find someone to take care of the baby for you?" she asked.

"Yes," said the princess.

Miriam ran home. "Mother! Mother! Come quick! The princess has found our baby. She needs someone to care for him."

Miriam and her mother hurried to the water. The princess said, "Please take care of this baby for me. I will pay you well."

Miriam and her mother took the baby. "Thank you,
God," Mother prayed, "for taking care of our baby boy."

Miriam and Aaron did not have to keep their baby brother a secret any longer.

They could giggle and laugh out loud. Pharaoh could never hurt their baby brother. God would always take care of him.

One day Mother took her little boy back to the princess. From then on Miriam and Aaron's little brother lived in the palace with the princess.

The princess was happy to have a little boy. And do you know what she named him?

Moses!

Obeying God at Jericho

Joshua, the leader of the Israelites, had a BIG problem. "We came here to the promised land because God told us to," he said. "But the big city of Jericho is in our way!"

From the camp of the Israelites, Joshua looked out at Jericho. The city had strong stone walls and tall gates locked up tight. This was a BIG problem, all right. Joshua sighed. If only he knew what to do next.

Joshua looked up. Someone was standing in front of him, holding a sparkling sword. Who was this?

Joshua walked closer. "Are you friend or foe?" he asked.

"Neither," said the visitor. "I have come as commander of the army of the Lord."

An angel! Joshua fell face down in front of the heavenly visitor. "Do you have a message for me from God?" Joshua asked.

"Take off your sandals," the angel said, "because you are standing in a holy place." So Joshua obeyed and listened to the angel.

Then Joshua told his men what the angel said. "We must march around the city once a day for six days. On the seventh day, we will march around the city seven times."

"Then the priests will blow their trumpets, and the people will shout! The walls of the city will tumble down.

"I know it is a strange way to fight a battle," Joshua said. "But this is God's battle, and we will obey God."

The priests and soldiers lined up right away and began to march. "*Shhh.* Don't say a word," Joshua told them. "Not until the day that I tell you to shout!"

Left, right, left, right. Joshua and the priests and soldiers marched around the city of Jericho. *Toot, toot-toot!* The sound of footsteps and trumpets was all that could be heard. No one said a word.

Left, right, left, right, all the way around the city.
Then Joshua, the priests, and the soldiers returned
to the camp. Every day for six days, they marched
around Jericho exactly as the commander of the
Lord's army had told them to do.

The people of Jericho watched from the top of the strong walls of their city and laughed. "Silly Israelites!" they shouted. "That's no way to fight a battle!"

But this was God's battle, and marching was what God wanted the Israelites to do. So Joshua and the people marched.

On the seventh day, just as the sun came up, the march around the city began again. One, two, three, four, five, six, seven times around the city the people marched. Then the priests blew a long blast on their trumpets—
toot, toot-TOOOOOOT!

"Give a mighty shout!" yelled Joshua. "For the Lord has given you the city!" The people SHOUTED!

Then, they heard a quiet *rrrrumble* . . .

The rumble grew louder. The strong walls of Jericho began to shake, and the tall locked gates began to rattle.

Then suddenly the city walls toppled with a *crash* and a *roar!*

83

Because they obeyed God, Joshua and the Israelites won the battle. They hurried into the city with cheers and shouts, thanking God for the victory.

DAVID AND GOLIATH

On one side of the valley stood the Philistine army. On the other side was the Israelite army, ready for battle. The two armies had been at war for years.

The Philistines had a champion warrior named Goliath. Goliath was over nine feet tall.

Every day Goliath stepped out to taunt the Israelites. He shouted in his booming voice, "If anyone is brave enough to fight me, let him step forward. If he defeats me, we will be your servants. If I defeat him, you will become our servants!"

When the Israelites heard the daring words of Goliath, they were afraid. No one was brave enough to fight Goliath.

David, a young shepherd boy, went to visit his older brothers who were in the Israelite army. He heard Goliath shouting at the Israelites as usual. He saw the Israelites run away, afraid to fight.

But David wasn't afraid. He volunteered to fight Goliath because no one else would. "You can't fight Goliath," King Saul told David. "He is a fighting champion, and you are just a boy!"

"God has helped me save my sheep from a lion and a bear. God will help me kill Goliath also," David replied.

King Saul blessed David and put his own armor on him. It was so heavy that David could hardly walk!

So David took off the armor. Then he chose five smooth stones from a stream, put them in his pouch, and went off to fight Goliath.

Goliath made fun of David. "Who do you think you are, coming to fight me? I am a champion Philistine warrior! You are only a boy!"

But David was not embarrassed or afraid. He knew that God was on his side.

When Goliath started to attack, David took a stone from his pouch and placed it in his sling. He whirled the sling above his head and let the stone fly through the air toward Goliath.

Thwock! The stone struck Goliath right in the middle of his forehead. Goliath fell to the ground, flat on his face.

The Philistines ran away in fear, and David became a hero to the Israelites.

David had defeated the giant. He knew that there is no problem too big for God!

Darius the Mede was king over all the land.

He chose 120 princes to rule under him. Then he chose three presidents to rule the princes.

Daniel was one of the presidents. King Darius liked Daniel the best because he was honest and did what was right.

All the other rulers were jealous of Daniel.

The other presidents and princes decided to catch Daniel in a mistake. But Daniel always worked hard, and he always did a good job.

"There is only one way we can get Daniel," one of the men said. "Listen! I have a plan. . . ."

Daniel's enemies went to see King Darius. "O king," they said, "we think you should make a law that says for 30 days no one may pray to any god or man except you. Anyone who breaks this law will be thrown into the lions' den. Sign here, Sire."

After Darius signed the law, Daniel's enemies said, "Now it is a law of the Medes and Persians. It can never be changed!"

Daniel knew about the new law. But God came first. Three times every day Daniel knelt and prayed to God.

"Aha!" cried Daniel's enemies. They had been watching Daniel. They ran to the king. "Daniel has broken your new law!" they said. "He must be thrown to the lions!"

The king was very upset. He liked Daniel. He tried all day to find a way to change the law.

At the end of the day, Daniel's enemies came back. "You know, O king, that the law of the Medes and Persians can never be changed."

King Darius had to call for Daniel. "May your God, whom you serve so well, save you," he said.

Soldiers threw Daniel down into the dark den. They put a big stone over the door and poured hot wax around it. The king pressed his signet ring in the wax so no one would open the door.

King Darius felt terrible. He didn't want any dinner or music. He worried about Daniel all night.

Finally, the sun came up. The king ran to the lions' den. *Was Daniel still alive?* "Daniel!" he called. "Has your God saved you?"

"God sent his angel to shut the lions' mouths," said Daniel. "Look! I am not even scratched!"

The king was very happy. So were the lions. The men who were Daniel's enemies were tossed into the lions' den, and the lions ate them for breakfast.

Then King Darius made a new law. It said, "Everyone must worship Daniel's God, for he is the living God. He saved Daniel in the lions' den."

Brave and Beautiful Queen Esther

Long ago there lived a young girl named Esther. Esther was raised by her older cousin Mordecai because both of her parents had died. As Esther grew up, she became more and more beautiful.

A time came when the king of the land was looking for a wife. Of all the girls in his kingdom, the king was most pleased with Esther. So she became queen.

Throughout history, queens have chosen the loveliest clothes, found the best beauty treatments, and, most importantly, learned the rules of the palace. So it was with Queen Esther. She dressed in beautiful gowns. She used delicious-smelling perfumes. And she learned the rules of her new home, the palace.

One important palace rule was: "Do not come to the king unless he calls you." If anyone, even the queen, displeased the king by breaking this rule, the person could be sentenced to death.

Perhaps this rule would not have mattered to Esther
if it had not been for a royal official named Haman.
Haman was a rich man and important. He
was also very proud. When the king gave
the command that people should bow
and honor Haman, Haman expected
everyone to do just that.

But Esther's cousin Mordecai would not bow down, and Haman became very, very angry! Soon Haman thought of a way to get rid of Mordecai. In fact, Haman planned to get rid of all of Mordecai's people.

Haman said to the king, "There is a certain group of people who live among us. They are different from us, and they do not obey our laws. Please issue a decree so that we may get rid of all these people."

Sadly, the king agreed to Haman's evil plan!

Now God's people were in terrible danger, for they were the ones Haman planned to destroy. When Esther heard of the plot, she was upset and afraid. No one in the palace knew Esther was one of God's people too.

Esther could not stand by and watch her people die. But what could she do? Esther asked all her friends to pray with her. She knew God could help her be brave.

Esther did not forget the palace rule: "Do not come to the king unless he calls you." But Esther had to speak to the king. She had to save her people. Esther decided to go against the palace rule.

"If I die, I die," Esther said. And she bravely walked into the king's throne room.

The king was pleased when he saw Esther standing before him. He extended his scepter to her. This was a sign that her life would be spared.

"What is your request?" asked the king.

"Grant me my life and spare my people," Esther said, "for our enemy Haman has a plot to destroy us all!"

When the king heard this, he immediately put an end to the evil plan against God's people and Haman was punished for trying to trick the king.

Esther was made queen because of her beauty. But it was because of her courage that God's people were saved.